AF445843

143 SOCIAL GENOCIDE PRACTICES IN ERDOGAN'S TURKEY

JULY 2022

ADVOCATES OF SILENCED TURKEY

AST is a 501(c)(3) Not for Profit charitable and educational organization based in NJ, exclusively for defending human and civil rights.

Our aim is, to address all forms of human rights violations being perpetrated in Turkey-- including civil, political, economic, social and cultural-- based on the tenets upheld in fundamental human rights documents;

To speak up against any forms of genocide, crimes against humanity, arbitrary detentions, cases of torture and ill treatment, and discrimination, and stand up for principles and values such as the right to life, the rule of law, the right to privacy, freedom of expression, freedom of thought, conscience and religion, and freedom of associations;

To utilize all human rights advocacy tools, mechanisms, and systems that can possibly be utilized in order to protect and demand the fundamental human rights of those whose voices are being silenced in Turkey and beyond;

And to hold accountable the perpetrators who are denying individuals in Turkey and beyond their fundamental Human Rights while providing the victims with the opportunity to obtain justice and reparation.

ADVOCATES OF SILENCED TURKEY

AST is a 501(c)(3) tax exempt, not for profit charitable and educational organization based in New Jersey, USA exclusively for defending human and civil rights.

EIN : 83-1568246

MAILING ADDRESS
Advocates of Silenced Turkey
P.O. Box 2399
Wayne, NJ 07474-2399

CONTACT
help@silencedturkey.org

WEB & SOCIAL MEDIA
www.silencedturkey.org
silencedturkey
facebook.com/silencedturkey
youtube.com/advocatesofsilencedturkey

AUTHOR
Deniz Kenan

PHOTO & DESIGN
Hamza Yormaz

EDITOR
Öznur Şahin

ASSİSTANT EDİTOR
Youssef Harvey

COVER DESIGN
Muhsin Nazif

CONTRIBUTIONS BY
Eda Kas, Murat Kaval

ACKNOWLEDGMENT AND DEDICATION

As AST, we extend our gratitude to the Union of the Platforms for KHK Victims that prepared the report "Social Costs of the State of Emergency", which identifies the rights violations and social genocide practices experienced by the victims of the **OHAL** and **KHK**s, whose number has reached 8 million, together with their families and relatives; to the late Prof. Dr. Haluk Savaş, who was a prominent human rights defender and a founder of the union. We commemorate and dedicate this study to the victims; to all the activists and rights defenders who announce unlawfulness to the public risking their lives and freedoms and provide material and moral support to the victims; fight against violations and run to heal the wounds, especially to Halime Gülsu, who lost her life in the prime of her youth after being arrested on the grounds of helping the victims, because she was not given her medicines in prison.

INTRODUCTION

This work presents an exhaustive list of flagrant human rights violations to the degree of social genocide, perpetrated after the coup attempt of 15 July 2016. The political Islamist and ultra-nationalist power bloc led by President Recep Tayyip Erdoğan has built an iron-fisted regime with the State of Emergency (OHAL) launched on July 21, 2016 and the consecutive, unsupervised statutory decrees (KHK). In this process, nearly 8 million people from all walks of life, including their families, were fired from their jobs, investigated, deprived of their freedom, ostracized from society, and almost driven to annihilation even though they had nothing to do with the coup.

Years before the coup attempt, dissidents were identified through unlawfully carried-out filings via the denunciations and unfettered and uncontrolled attainments of civil authorities, intelligence and even ordinary people. With the aforementioned profiling, 152,000 civil servants were dismissed from their duties without even taking their statements for their critical views about the government or for their affiliations with the Hizmet movement. Institutions and workplaces known to be close to Hizmet were closed, and nearly 200,000 employees were dismissed, deprived of all their inalienable rights.

Although there is an attempt to create a perception in the public opinion of Turkey and the world that the decree laws were issued solely for the purpose of dismissals, the actual situation was far more different than that. Turkey's political Islamist and ultra-nationalist government bloc has in effect purportedly abused the KHKs for a number of various "social genocide" methods against the Hizmet members and critical figures such as abduction, enforced disappearance, torture, long detention, years of solitary confinement, social isolation, marginalization, dehumanization and demonization. The violations of rights and social genocide practices to which the OHAL and KHK victims are subjected differ according to the arbitrariness and discrimination of the officials in the places the victims live or in the public and social areas they apply to.

Within this framework, the report identified 143 rights violations and social genocide practices. Since some of these practices are executed publicly, it is known to everyone. We have noted some of them during research and interviews. The fact that many violations of rights were noticed in this way shows the possibility that there may be many more violations of rights that have not yet been identified. In this regard, the study of rights violations will be updated in future editions with new applications and new findings.

WHAT DOES KHK MEAN?

✖ KHK does not only mean being expelled from public service and losing the right to work.

✖ KHK means being designated as a member of a terrorist organization and dismissed without question just because of the membership of a union, depositing money in a bank, having critical views against the government, fighting for labor, democracy and peace, or simply because of a different belief. It means the continuation of the state of emergency and a new form of government.

✖ KHK means the suspension of the constitution, laws, the law, human rights, international agreements, and an overwhelming disregard of the most basic citizenship and human rights.

✖ KHKs mean ignoring the right to defense, the presumption of innocence, the right to have an unblemished reputation, and the right to be tried in accordance with universal law impartially.

✖ KHK means the silencing of those whom political power perceives as a threat to its own power; it entails closing newspapers and magazines, destroying institutions, and, in short, silencing the opposition..

✖ KHK refers to the administration of trustees who are appointed rather than elected. KHK is an abbreviation for nepotism, bribery, plunder, pillage and availing public benefits exclusively to cronies.

✖ KHK denotes the robbing of individuals' freedoms and professions as well as their past, present and future, condemning them to political captivity and starvation, civilian death and prison.

✖ KHK is an acronym that stands for usurpation of job security and vested rights. It means intimidating people with security investigations and using threats of unemployment and incarceration to suppress those who have their freedom and job. It means bringing an affliction not only on individuals, but also on future generations descended from them, and chastising them all.

✖ KHK entails the expulsion of thousands of academics from the academy who stated that they would not participate in this crime because they desired peace.

✖ KHK means severe and systematic torture by the state itself.

✖ KHK means handcuffs. It means suicide. It means death. It means more than 100 suicides, 700 deaths from diseases, 864 babies growing up in prison, 17,000 women, more than 100,000 political prisoners.

✖ KHK means cadets who were sentenced to life imprisonment on the charge of attempting a coup d'etat when they were only teenagers.

✖ KHK refers to the case that has been examined by the delay commission for 6 years, reinstatement after death, arbitrary refusal decisions and prolongation of the court process.

✖ KHK means turning people asylees in their homelands, by the exploitation of 143 violations of rights such as not having the right to be elected and opening the right to vote for discussion.

✖ KHK entails that corruption becomes the new law of the land; it connotes children who have to grow up in prison because their mothers are locked behind bars.

✖ KHK means drowning in Meriç river and Aegean sea for those who want to escape, and being shackled in prisons for those who stay despite everything.

✖ KHK means Leviathan's abuse of the tyrannical power to protect itself and the fortification of the one-man regime.

✖ KHK means to stifle demands for democracy, freedom, equality, justice and human rights; It means making the country a thornless rose garden for corrupt political power.

CONTENTS

Right to life

- ▷ **Push to death**
- ▷ **Actual assault and incitement to murder**
- ▷ **Causing death via psychological attacks**
- ▷ **Causing death via economic barriers**
- ▷ **Forcing to suicide**
- ▷ **Causing women to commit suicide**
- ▷ **Causing children to commit suicide**
- ▷ **Causing elderly to commit suicide**
- ▷ **Causing the suicide of people with disabilities**
- ▷ **Causing women's death**
- ▷ **Causing children's death**
- ▷ **Causing the death of the elderly**
- ▷ **Causing the death of the people with disabilities**
- ▷ **Attempting to silence victims with assassinations**
- ▷ **Forcing people to death in prisons**

 *Push to death*

People were driven to death mainly by indirect means, making the social genocide committed by the KHKs on and after July 20, 2016 more subtle, more difficult to prove and to facilitate its denial by the perpetrators. Premeditated murders remained in limited numbers.

Many people have become unable to sustain their lives due to practices such as barring from working, prevention of social benefits and any form of social solidarity, malnutrition, hunger, imprisonment, usurpation of property rights, bans from the profession, prevention of commercial activities, and prevention of health services. These activities were not only carried out by almost all public institutions such as the judiciary, the police, intelligence, Social Security Institution (SGK), financial auditors, but also companies and institutions from the private sector participated in the social extermination campaign, either by state pressure or by their own will.

As a result, thousands of people lost their lives because of the health issues they had due to malnutrition, lack of livelihood, grief and stress, or from suicide as a result of depression. There were some who died on the death fast, which they resorted to out of desperation. Mothers, their children, pregnant women and their unborn babies lost their lives due to practices such as detention and solitary confinement or to deliberate neglect of health care. Again, many victims died in prisons due to deprivation of health care, prevention or delay of the delivery of medication, or not being released despite their terminal illnesses.

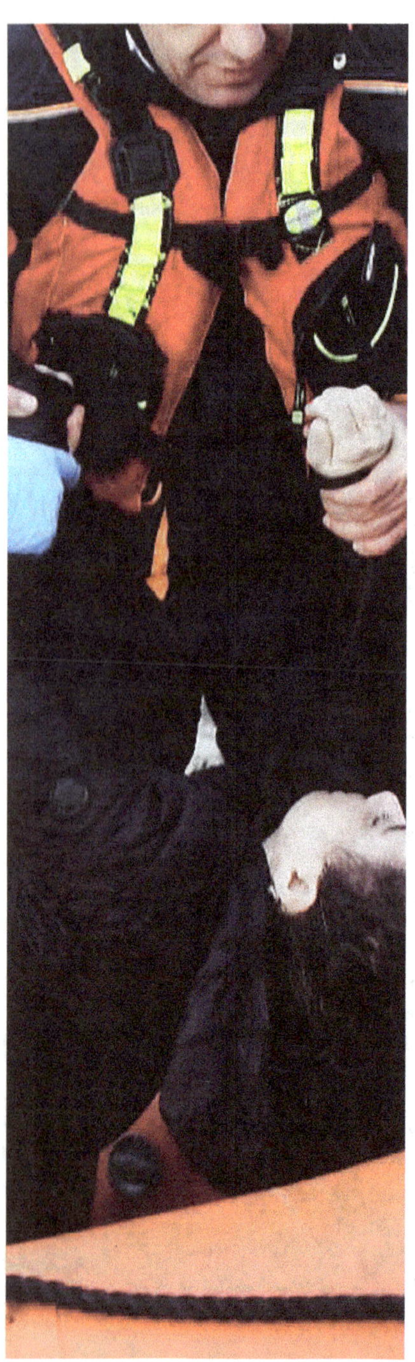

2 Actual assault and incitement to murder

Soldiers, cadets or civilians were killed in front of the cameras by murder, lynching and sniper shots. There were actual attacks and killings, mostly by torture, in many places. Article 121 of Decree Law No. 696 stated that "Provisions of paragraph 1 [immunity] shall also be applicable to those individuals who acted with the aim of suppressing the coup attempt and the terrorist activities that took place on July 15, 2016 and actions that can be deemed as the continuation of these, without having regard to whether they held an official title or were performing an official duty or not." This was interpreted as a license to kill and thanks to these regulations, the criminals were taken under the protection of the state, so the prosecutor's office decided not to prosecute torture and murder. Thus, the murders and tortures of both public officials and people under the auspices of the political power were placed under the protection of the state.

3 Causing death via psychological attacks

OHAL and KHK victims have been labeled as terrorists by the political power although none of their acts constitute crime according to the current laws. Again, intense propaganda of the government through the media under its control and influence provoked and agitated the masses against these people. In the consequent atmosphere, the victims, contrary to all religious, national, moral and political values, were slandered and demonized with lies and through intimidation, isolation, humiliation and incitement, and were exposed to a social lynching. These people, who were stigmatized with accusations such as terrorists and traitors, could not find a job, were exposed to hunger and diseases with their families, were left alone and psychologically devastated, and left in the grip of severe illness and death.

4 Causing death via economic barriers

All sorts of financial aid to the spouses and children of the detainees/convicts were prevented, and even those who provided food aid to these people were arrested on charges of supporting terrorism. Families, who were prevented from finding a job, were deprived of help from benevolent people and even from their relatives, and their health deteriorated further due to factors such as hunger and neglect, thus they were pushed to death deliberately.

Codes 36 or 38 were registered in the SGK record of the victims and their relatives. Thus, it has been ensured that even the children of the victims will be affected by the social genocide. The fact that these codes are posted to the SGK proves that the target in genocide is not only the person himself, but other people who have ties of marriage and kinship with the person.

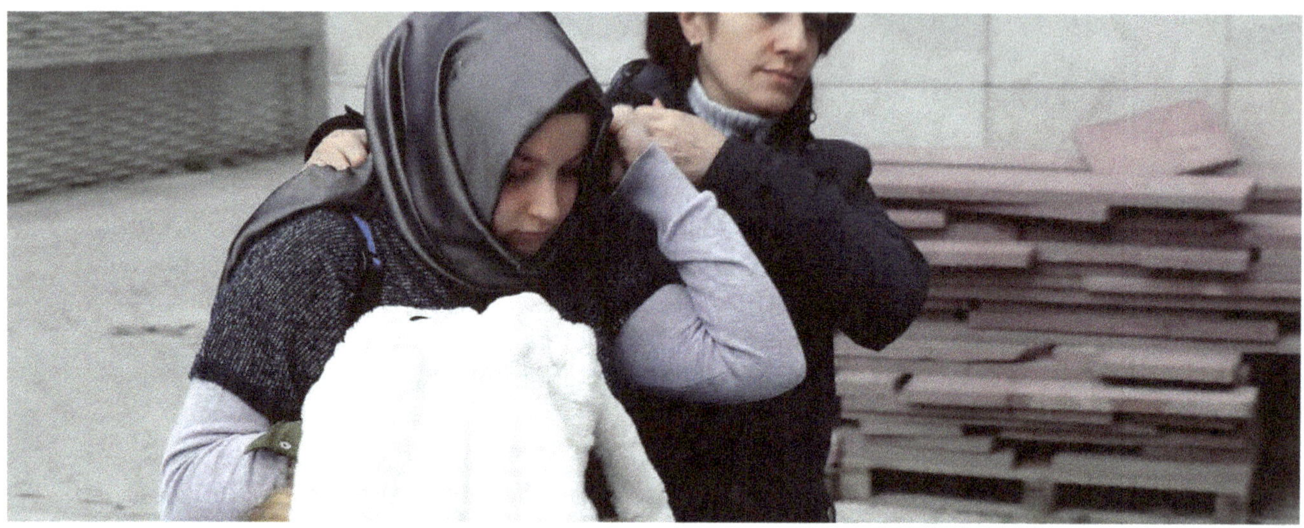

5 Forcing to suicide

In addition to the actual killings, many KHK victims and their relatives were forced to commit suicide due to the social lynching atmosphere created in the society in line with the genocidal practices of the political power, and the systematic pressure and torture in prisons. There are around 100 cases of suicide among the victims of the KHK and their relatives. However, the actual numbers are thought to be much higher than these figures. On the other hand, even the current figures reflected to the public are well above the suicide rates in Turkey. As evidence of the intention to deliberately cause the suicides of many by decree laws, there are statements of victims that after the severe torture they suffered, their torturers "left suicide tools in places where they can see and reach" in order to force them or make it easier for them to commit suicide. As a result, the high rates of suicide among the KHK victims showed that the efforts to force the victims and their relatives, who were left in the dead-end of the 'death corridor', to commit suicide by systematically blocking all life channels socially and economically have been successful to some extent.

 6 Causing women to commit suicide

As a result of psychological and social pressures during the OHAL regime, women who were KHK victims or relatives of victims could not stand the marginalization, hostility, defamation and unlawfulness they experienced and committed suicide. For example, a mother of 3 children, Sevgi Balcı, who was expelled from the nursing profession and whose husband is imprisoned, could not stand the violations of her rights and committed suicide.

 7 Causing children to commit suicide

As a result of psychological and social pressures during the OHAL regime, children who were relatives of the KHK victims committed suicide due to the marginalization and hostility they experienced. For example, Bahadır Kandemir, whose father was a political prisoner, could not cope with the traumas he experienced and died at the age of 16 by committing suicide.

8 *Causing elderly to commit suicide*

Psychological and social pressures caused by the ruthless practices of the OHAL regime have led to the suicide of the elderly KHK victims or the elderly relatives of the victims. In addition to the studies conducted through social media, studies conducted by AST have found that many elderly people committed suicide as a result of suddenly appearing diseases, abruptly worsening of their existing diseases or depression.

9 *Causing the suicide of people with disabilities*

Many practices that made life unlivable under OHAL such as breaking up the families of KHK victims, condemning them to hunger and despair by destroying their economic income sources as well as social lynching and isolation pushed the disabled, whose lives were already filled with great difficulties, into severe depressions and led them to commit suicide.

 10 Causing women's death

As a result of deliberate practices of delaying or preventing treatment during the state of emergency regime, many female the KHK victims or their female relatives died. Some of the women who were arrested while pregnant and deprived not only of their freedom but also of access to health services at the most critical time, lost their lives.

 11 Causing children's death

Due to the OHAL the regime practices, children of many the KHK victims and of their relatives lost their lives as a result of delaying or preventing their treatment.

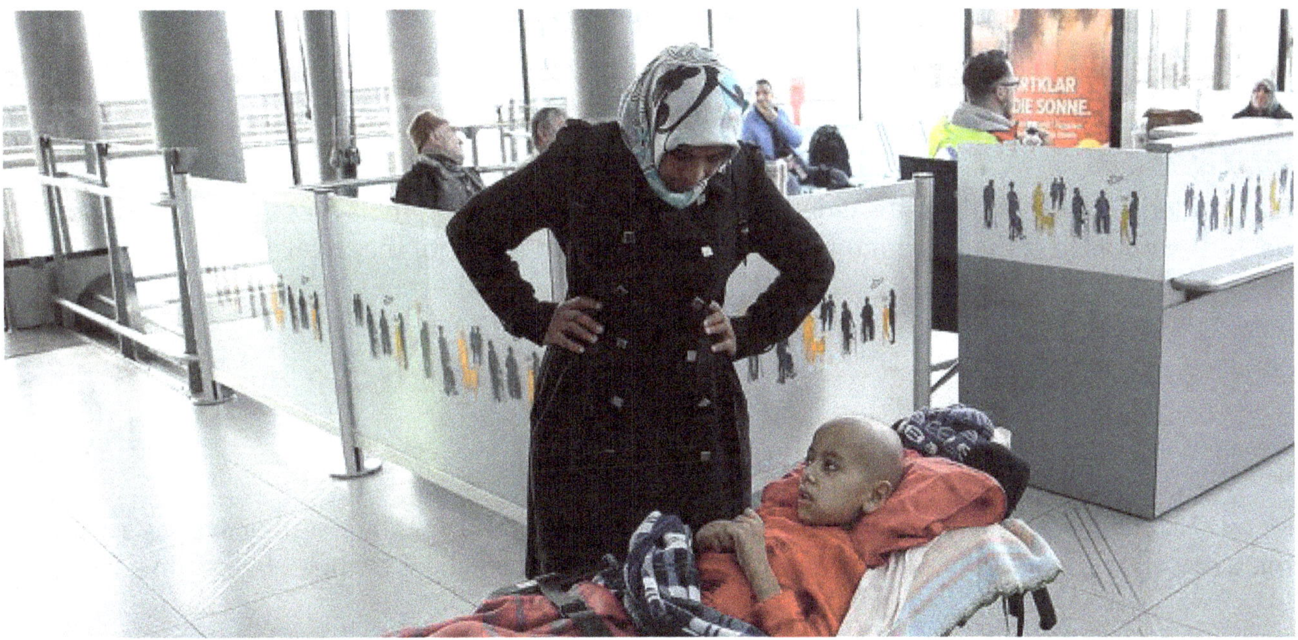

12 *Causing the death of the elderl*

Many elderly KHK victims and the elderly relatives of the victims lost their lives as a result of the delay or hindrance of their treatment due to the ruthless practices of the OHAL regime.

13 *Causing the death of the people with disabilities*

Many KHK victims with disabilities or the disabled relatives of the victims lost their lives as a result of the delay or hindrance of their treatment due to the ruthless practices of the OHAL regime.

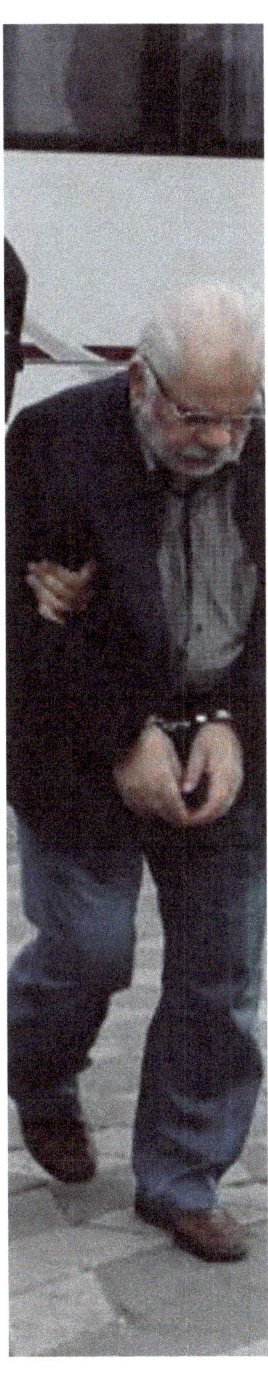

14 Attempting to silence victims with assassinations

The KHK victims, who are likely to reveal some information against the perpetrators of genocide in prisons or outside, are silenced by the assassins. For example, businessman Hazım Sesli was stabbed with a skewer in prison after stating during a trial in the court, "I know a lot, I know about current ministers and past ministers. I haven't spoken until now, but if I do, the ground will shake. I demand this to be known."

15 Forcing people to death in prisons

Victims in prison are trying to survive in unbearable conditions amidst isolation and ill treatment to an extent that is not even applied to common criminals. Some of them lost their lives due to the harsh prison conditions, their treatment being blocked, their medication not being given, or the fact that they were not allowed to be released despite their terminal illnesses.

Indeed, the number of sick prisoners in need of care in prisons is expressed in the thousands, and there are detainees whose disease severity is substantiated with medical reports. Although it was clearly stated in the health committee reports issued by the authorized health boards for some prisoners that their lives were in danger, that they cannot live on their own given the prison conditions, that they were in constant need of someone else's care, that their illness was continuous, and that therefore, the the sentence must be postponed. However, the court committees deprived many prisoners of their liberty and right to treatment and essential care.

Prohibition of Torture and Ill-Treatment

- ▷ **Systematic torture and ill-treatment**
- ▷ **Forced disappearances**
- ▷ **Abductions from abroad and renditions**
- ▷ **Legitimizing harassment, rape and systematic torture**

16 *Systematic torture and ill-treatment*

The KHK victims were subjected to torture and ill-treatment in detention, interrogation and prisons. According to the testimonies of the victims, who had the opportunity to speak later, the torture was mostly carried out to force the victims to accept prefabricated statements, to prevent them from seeking their rights, to intimidate them or sometimes just to oppress them. Torturers have almost gained the armor of immunity, for example the license vested by the Article 121 of Decree Law No. 696, and prosecutors and judges simply ignored the allegations of torture especially towards political prisoners. This, in turn, encouraged inhuman practices and ensured their continuation.

17 *Forced disappearances*

The Turkish intelligence abducted and forcibly disappeared the opponents, especially some former public officials and teachers, who were members of the Hizmet movement, through clandestine operations in the country. These people were subjected to severe torture for months and then handed over to the police illegally mostly after having them forcibly sign pre-prepared false statements, implicating certain people. Some people who were abducted in broad daylight by masked people in black Transporter vehicles could not be heard from for years. There are strong suspicions that these people were killed.

18 *Abductions from abroad and renditions*

The Turkish state not only suppressed the dissidents in the country through inhuman enforced disappearances, but also tried to bring the dissidents living in other countries to the country illegally, by kidnapping or by diplomatic pressure for their deportation. Especially countries where democratic institutions have not developed and which are backward in terms of the rule of law, surrendered to the pressures of the Erdoğan regime and handed over the dissidents living within their frontiers to Turkey, in a flagrant breach of international law. As seen most recently in the abduction of Orhan İnandı from Kyrgyztan, dozens of people were kidnapped by the MİT and forced to sign confessions imposed on them under heavy torture.

19 *Legitimizing harassment, rape and systematic torture*

There have been numeroeus incidents of rape, especially in prisons, reported by the victims at courts during trials or to international human rights organizations' delegations. During some hearings, the judges silenced the victims as they were describing how they were raped, saying that "this issue has nothing to do with your defense", thus covering up the crime of torture. Likewise, investigation requests of international human rights organizations were not heeded and the perpetrators of crimes were somehow protected.

The tortures inflicted on some victims in front of their spouses and children led to the moral collapse of family members, especially children, and to the serious destruction of their social relations. With the traumas caused by this, families were broken up, and there were cases of suicide among adults and children who lost their mental health.

Right to Security and Reputation Protection

- ▷ Systematic black propaganda
- ▷ Systematic purge with profiling lists
- ▷ Condoning to crimes
- ▷ Lynching at national and international levels
- ▷ Social lynching
- ▷ Mobbing students at schools because of their parents
- ▷ Mobbing through ties of kinship
- ▷ Mobbing over distant kinship ties
- ▷ Systematic hypocrisy and abuse
- ▷ Attacks on personality and spiritual integrity
- ▷ Attacks on social identity and statuses
- ▷ Accusation of coup and filing of families of those who died before July 15
- ▷ Demotion and hierarchical discrediting
- ▷ Resetting their professional careers
- ▷ Destroying hopes for the future
- ▷ Denial of testimony

20 Systematic black propaganda

The political power has continuously carried out smear campaigns in the print media and social media, deliberately demonizing dissidents as well as the Hizmet movement in the eyes of the public, with accusations and insults such as traitors, hashashis and terrorists. Their names were vilified, dishonored and stigmatized by being labeled "terrorist" in the supplementary lists of the Decree Laws published in the Official Gazette. The 'right not to be tainted', one of the most basic principles of human rights, has been violated.

4	HALIS TUNÇ	1. DERECE AILE FERTLERININ (EŞ-ÇOCUK HARICINDE) [...]	
8	RESUL MÜLAYIM	EŞININ 2010/100074 SORUSTURMA SAYISINA KAYDEN YÜRÜTÜLEN KPSS SORUŞTURMASI ŞÜPHELISI OLDUĞU	
2	FEHMI KARAAĞAÇ	1. DERECE AILE FERTLERININ (EŞ-ÇOCUK HARICINDE) BANKASYA MEVDUATI OLDUĞU	Vasington JSF Gbrou Sls. ve EH ✓
2	FEHMI KARAAĞAÇ	1. DERECE AILE FERTLERININ (EŞ-ÇOCUK HARICINDE) BANKASYA MEVDUATI OLDUĞU	
8	SUAT TOSUN	1. DERECE AILE FERTLERININ (EŞ-ÇOCUK HARICINDE) BANKASYA MEVDUATI OLDUĞU	
0	MEHMET EMIN TOMAS	EŞININ 2010/100074 SORUSTURMA SAYISINA KAYDEN YÜRÜTÜLEN KPSS SORUŞTURMASI ŞÜPHELISI OLDUĞU	Varşova As. Ats. ✓
0	MEHMET EMIN TOMAS	EŞININ PDY/FETÖ ILIŞIK KAYDI BULUNDUĞU	
2	HARUN DEMIRTAŞ	1. DERECE AILE FERTLERININ (EŞ-ÇOCUK HARICINDE) BANKASYA MEVDUATI OLDUĞU	
0	GÖKHAN MERMERTAŞ	PDY/FETÖ MENSUBU ÜST DÜZEY ŞAHIS (MÜTEVELLI, DERNEK BAŞKANI VS) ADINA KAYITLI GSM IL IRTIBATLI	
6	UĞUR AKYAZI	1. DERECE AILE FERTLERININ (EŞ-ÇOCUK HARICINDE) BANKASYA MEVDUATI OLDUĞU	
4	MAHMUT ÖZÇETIN	PDY/FETÖ MENSUBU ÜST DÜZEY ŞAHIS (MÜTEVELLI, DERNEK BAŞKANI VS) ADINA KAYITLI GSM IL IRTIBATLI	
2	SEFA DEMIREL	EŞININ PDY/FETÖ ILTISAKLI KURUMLARDA SGK KAYDININ BULUNDUĞU	
2	SEFA DEMIREL	EŞININ 2010/100074 SORUSTURMA SAYISINA KAYDEN YÜRÜTÜLEN KPSS SORUŞTURMASI ŞÜPHELISI OLDUĞU	
2	SEFA DEMIREL	EŞININ PDY/FETÖ ILTISAKLI KURUMLARDA SGK KAYDININ BULUNDUĞU	
0	ALI KAYA	1. DERECE AILE FERTLERININ (EŞ-ÇOCUK HARICINDE) PDY/FETÖ ILTISAKLI SENDIKALARA ÜYE OLDUĞU	
0	ALI KAYA	EŞININ BANKASYA MEVDUATI OLDUĞU	
0	MUSA SAĞLIK	1. DERECE AILE FERTLERININ (EŞ-ÇOCUK HARICINDE) BANKASYA MEVDUATI OLDUĞU	Saraybosna As.Ats. Yrd. (Eğt
4	HÜSEYIN SARPKAYA	1. DERECE AILE FERTLERININ (EŞ-ÇOCUK HARICINDE) BANKASYA MEVDUATI OLDUĞU	
8	MUSTAFA SONER KARTOP	1. DERECE AILE FERTLERININ (EŞ-ÇOCUK HARICINDE) BANKASYA MEVDUATI OLDUĞU	Vasington Kara Ats. Yrd. (Kara
8	MUSTAFA SONER KARTOP	1. DERECE AILE FERTLERININ (EŞ-ÇOCUK HARICINDE) BANKASYA MEVDUATI OLDUĞU	
0	AYHAN EKER	EŞININ PDY/FETÖ ILTISAKLI KURUMLARDA SGK KAYDININ BULUNDUĞU	
0	AYHAN EKER	PDY/FETÖ MENSUBU ÜST DÜZEY ŞAHIS (MÜTEVELLI, DERNEK BAŞKANI VS) ADINA KAYITLI GSM IL IRTIBATLI	
6	YASIN YAVUZ	EŞININ 2010/100074 SORUSTURMA SAYISINA KAYDEN YÜRÜTÜLEN KPSS SORUŞTURMASI ŞÜPHELISI OLDUĞU	
0	CEVDET YAŞAR	EŞININ 2010/100074 SORUSTURMA SAYISINA KAYDEN YÜRÜTÜLEN KPSS SORUŞTURMASI ŞÜPHELISI OLDUĞU	Tiflis As.Ats.
0	CEVDET YAŞAR	1. DERECE AILE FERTLERININ (EŞ-ÇOCUK HARICINDE) BANKASYA MEVDUATI OLDUĞU	
8	BURHAN AYDIN	1. DERECE AILE FERTLERININ (EŞ-ÇOCUK HARICINDE) PDY/FETÖ ILTISAKLI KURUMLARDAN SSK KAYDI BULUNDUĞU	
8	BURHAN AYDIN	1. DERECE AILE FERTLERININ (EŞ-ÇOCUK HARICINDE) BANKASYA MEVDUATI OLDUĞU	
8	BURHAN AYDIN	EŞININ PDY/FETÖ ILTISAKLI KURUMLARDA SGK KAYDININ BULUNDUĞU	
	...AYHAN ALTINKAYNAK	EŞININ PDY/FETÖ ILTISAKLI KURUMLARDA EĞITIM GÖRDÜĞÜ	

21 Systematic purge with profiling lists

Lists published right after the coup attempt indicate that the names of the KHK victims were determined long ago through illegal filing. Later, in addition to the provincial and district organizations and party members of the ruling party, tens of thousands of people from the public and private sectors such as state officials, bureaucrats, members of the MIT and the police were employed in this comprehensive filing operation. Thus, long before July 2016, they prepared purge lists for dissidents.

With a method called FETÖMETRE, which was developed within the military to determine who is a member of the Hizmet movement and based on completely subjective and baseless criteria, more than 40,000 members of the army were expelled. FETÖMETRE is one of the most important tools for preparing tagging lists with constantly changing criteria. This method, which allows the managers at public institutions to arbitrarily select any dissident civil servant to append to purge lists, has been widely used in the purges of the police, judges, prosecutors and the state bureaucracy.

22 Condoning to crimes

Criminal complaints and denunciations by the victims that they were harassed or raped were not taken into account on the grounds that 'the allegations by the people branded with terrorism is not taken into account.' Thus, those who commit crimes against the victims were favored. The violation of the rights is legitimized and even encouraged and facilitated by depriving the victims of the legal and constitutional protections enjoyed by every citizen.

23 Lynching at national and international levels

Public officials, pro-government journalists and trolls in print and visual media and social media organized social and psychological lynchings in an organized and systematic way to discredit the OHAL and KHK victims. With fake indictments prepared according to fake news spinned by trolls on social media, people were put on the terrorist lists, and even the names of some people were recorded as terrorists in the database of media such as Interpol, and a monetary reward was promised for their heads.

24 · Social lynching

With the campaigns organized against the KHK victims and with the encouragement and organization of the government, their relatives, acquaintances and neighbors carried out a social lynching against the KHK victims. For example, Emine Özdemir Kara, who was expelled with her brother by KHK in Eskişehir, was subjected to insults and bullying by all the people of the neighborhood, such as forcibly collecting garbage on the street.

25 · Mobbing students at schools because of their parents

In some schools, students have been labeled as "the son/daughter of a terrorist", isolated and marginalized by the school administration, teachers, students and parents. Some teachers humiliated these children in front of their schoolmates, causing them to suffer psychological trauma.

26 *Mobbing through ties of kinship*

Mobbing was applied to the spouse, children and-or relatives of the victim through ties of kinship. Those who had people close to the Hizmet movement among their relatives were oppressed by the society just for this reason, and they were subjected to social pressure because they did not cut their kinship relations with these people. Those who tried to defend their relatives were even accused of being "terrorists" or "traitors". Investigations were launched against them and they were threatened to be imprisoned should they not stop backing their relatives.

27 *Mobbing over distant kinship ties*

The mobbing described above was not only limited to the first-degree relatives of the KHK victims, but also to their second- and third-degree relatives.

28 *Systematic hypocrisy and abuse*

KHK victims participated in exam, election or certificate programs by paying their fees, but were barred from their rights even though they successfully completed the exams or programs or won the elections. For example, municipal committees or headmen could not get their mandates despite winning the elections. For instance, the government forcibly removed the mayors who won the election as candidates from the HDP and appointed people close to the ruling party as trustees. Some of the victims, who were labeled as terrorism and treason, were drafted into the military, and those who were martyred during their military service were buried with a state ceremony.

29 *Attacks on personality and spiritual integrity*

Victims saw systematic attacks on their identities and personalities, sustaining serious damages to their psychological wellbeing and character integrity. In numerous instances, to force victims to sign prefabricated statements, the torturers threatened them with their spouses, children, their own honor, and the honor of their spouses and daughters. They kept some victims in solitary cells for months even years, trying to break their moral resistance. As part of the practices of extermination, the rights to obtain a job, to receive education, to access health services, and to access many other public services have been arbitrarily denied.

SAĞLIK BAKANLIĞI

SIRA NO	ADI SOYADI	GÖREV YERİ/GÖREVİ	TANIDANSI	BİLGİ TARİHİ
1	Abdullah KURŞUN	Mardin Sağlık Memuru	I.YILDIRIM Grubu Nurcu	Mayıs 1997
2	Abdullah TUĞRUL	Edirne	Nakşibendi	Ocak 1997
3	Abdullah YASİN	Edirne	F.GÜLEN Grubu Nurcu	Haziran 1999
4	Adil KAYA	Sivas Hast.Doktor	Mazlum-Der	1997
5	Adil YILMAYAN	Ş.Urfa İl Sağlık Md.Eğt. Şb. Md.	İzzettin YILDIRIM Grubu Nurcu	Eylül 1999
6	Adile YEŞİLDAĞ	Konya/C.Beyli Kuşça Sağ.Oca.	Genel İslamcı	Kasım 1999

 Attacks on social identity and statuses

With widespread hate speech, a systematic smear campaign was launched against people who were respected in the society due to their social and economic status until 15 July 2016. With dozens of insulting accusations against these people, such as 'traitor', 'terrorist', 'enemy of the state', 'enemy of the nation' and 'pervert', the social reputation, social status and social identities of the victims have been severely damaged.

 Accusation of coup and filing of families of those who died before July 15

The names of individuals who died or even soldiers who became martyrs before July 15, 2016 were published on the KHK lists of expelled officers. They were included in the investigation files by prosecutor offices and were accused of taking part in the coup attempt. The relatives of the deceased public officers were profiled and barriers were erected against them.

 Demotion and hierarchical discrediting

Even if the KHK victims were later reinstated to their positions, this time hierarchical discrediting was performed.

33 Resetting their professional careers

The social and cultural genocidal practices of isolating the person from the society and destroying their reputation were not limited to a certain period of time. The names of the victims have been deleted from the histories, publications and websites of the institutions they used to work for, or their past contributions and experiences have been obliterated. All their education and graduation records were terminated and their vocational certificates were revoked, and the discipline and experience they have gained by working for years has been wasted.

34 Destroying hopes for the future

Not only have the past career, experience and knowledge been taken away from the victims, but also their expectations and hopes for the future have been destroyed. Their chance to be successful in education is prevented through arbitrary restrictions or mobbing. It is rendered difficult for them to find a decent job. They are discredited in society. Everywhere they apply, they encounter a security investigation and even if there is a person with a KHK among their family members or relatives, they face obstacles. Above all, all these troubles become permanent due to the records in their registry.

35 Denial of testimony

The victims of the KHK are registered as "unfavorable persons" or "risky persons" in the databases of the Banking Regulation and Supervision Agency, General Directorate of Land Registry and Cadastre, Ministry of Interior, Turkish Employment Agency etc. Any person with this registry was denied in and prevented from participating in official proceedings as witnesses.

Freedom of Thought and Expression

- ▷ **Obstruction of self-expression**
- ▷ **Violation of the right to information**
- ▷ **Silencing with the threat of administrative fine**

 36 *Obstruction of self-expression*

Through the suppression of the press and the obstruction of the right to information in public organizations, the ways of obtaining information at individual and public levels have been blocked. Journalists were targeted on many occasions and were deprived of their passports, press cards, jobs and even retirement, without any judicial or administrative action against them and without even knowing what they were accused of. With the silencing of the critical media, the social media emerged as the only place where the victims of the genocide can make their voices heard. However, even in this medium, there was no opportunity for completely free and unhindered expression due to the clamp down on these platforms like vigilante media elements and trolls under the control of the government and the Criminal Judgeships of Peace.

37 *Violation of the right to information*

The right of press members, victims and their lawyers to receive information from official institutions has been severely hindered during the OHAL and the restrictions still linger even today. Thus, the right to receive information from public institutions has been usurped.

 38 *Silencing with the threat of administrative fine*

Administrative fines were exploited as a tool to silence dissenting voices. Victims were detained while seeking their rights peacefully by speaking up about the injustice while walking on a street or sitting on a bench. Deterrent and repetitive fines were imposed on those who were marked in this way, and their use of their democratic right to protest was substantially restricted.

Freedom of Religion and Conscience

▷ **Restriction of religious freedom and excommunication**
▷ **Restriction of performing Hajj**
▷ **Prohibition of fasting**
▷ **Prevention from entering mosques**

39 Restriction of religious freedom and excommunication

Clerics who are in the same mindset as the government and who have a certain position in the society as well as the zealots who believe in their words have yelled out in streets such religiously-inspired slogans like "their bodies are carrion [meaning killing them is not a sin], their wives are halal [meaning sexually assaulting their wives is not a sin], their goods are booty [meaning plundering their properties is not a sin]". In some places they were denied basic ceremonies socially and religiously required for the deceased like funeral processions and prayers, gasil [washing and cleaning the corpse] and burial [shrouding in white cloth and burying with prayers]. Some imams and people said the people whom the political power of a state expelled with KHKs had no place in the Muslim cemeteries. Victims in prisons were prevented from reading the Qur'an and religious books. Even the books in the prison libraries were not given to them with arbitrary restrictions by the higher authorities. In some places, the requests of the prisoners to get a clean mat for prayer was turned down.

40 Restriction of performing Hajj

Victims and their relatives were prevented from performing pilgrimage visits to Mecca as a result of their passports being revoked and their applications for new passports rejected. Violation of the right to travel for religious purposes was not limited to only the victims of the KHKs, but was also arbitrarily applied to their relatives.

41 Prohibition of fasting

Prison administrations and prison and detention center officers didn't provide facilities when detainees and prisoners wanted to fast. Fasting people were sentenced to arbitrary solitary confinement and were deprived of food and water for iftar.

42 Prevention from entering mosques

In some places, KHK victims who are known to have affiliations with the Hizmet movement were prevented from entering mosques to pray. They and their families were told, "You are terrorists. Allah refuses your prayers and you cannot pray in our mosques", and these people were expelled from mosques.

Right to a Fair Trial

- ▷ Violation of the right to a fair trial
- ▷ Violation of the Principle of Equality
- ▷ Arbitrariness and discrimination
- ▷ Presumption of guilt
- ▷ Violation of rights to defense or to access defense
- ▷ Arbitrary restriction of freedom
- ▷ Unsubstantiated allegations
- ▷ Restriction of complaints and defense rights
- ▷ Retrospective laws
- ▷ Ignoring the principle of individual criminal responsibility
- ▷ Specially authorized courts
- ▷ Sentencing beforehand and looking for evidence later
- ▷ Holding family members hostage
- ▷ Deadlock between the commission and the project courts
- ▷ Ill-treatment in detention and under arrest
- ▷ Discrimination in penalty relief and forcing to give up legal rights
- ▷ Political pressure on judicial and administrative institutions
- ▷ Failure to comply with judicial decisions in favor of the victim
- ▷ Alienating victims in prison

43 | *Violation of the right to a fair trial*

The rights of the KHK victims to a fair trial have been violated in a planned and systematic way through such heinous methods like false testimony, fabrication of false statements and expert reports in administrative investigations, spoliation of the evidence in favor of the KHK victims in official records, not providing the information and documents they need when requested, dissemination of false information through news channels to the public, tampering with the autopsy/expert reports to hide the truth, not providing crime scene camera footages, destruction of favorable evidence, the obscuring of the evidence against certain groups with power and their descendants, the extermination of important witnesses by killing them, presenting some murders with snipers as if they were committed by the victims of the social genocide, covering up the crime or shifting the blame to the KHK victims or the Hizmet movement in cases when the culprit is from the privilege power groups or from the ruling party, ignoring the criminal complaints against perpetrators of torture.

44 | *Violation of the Principle of Equality*

KHK victims that were targeted in violation of the principle of 'Equal Protection Before the Law' were exposed to situations such as organized fraud, concealment of evidence, spoliation of evidence and fabrication of false evidence, in order that they could not defend themselves and be convicted.

45 *Arbitrariness and discrimination*

The accusations against the critics of the government and the victims of the KHKs were arbitrary and that they were discriminated against by ignoring the basic principle of equality before the law.

Courts and public institutions making decisions on these people used the profiling lists and relied on the arbitrariness of the people who prepared these lists while deciding which acts are crimes, according to which criteria the penalty was imposed, who is guilty and who is innocent, who is trustworthy and loyal to the state and who is a traitor. Under an arbitrarily and subjectively determined criteria, dissidents were accused and convicted of acts that are not defined as crimes in the law. They were tried in heavy penal courts and sentenced to tens of years, ignoring the principle of "no crime and punishment without law". Some of these actions are as follows: Having an account at Bank Asya, which operated with the permission of and under the control of the state's relevant bodies; being a member of the Active Educators Union, which operated completely legally within the scope of constitutional rights; to have sent their child to some private schools affiliated to the Ministry of National Education; to have used the smartphone application ByLock which was freely available at app stores of Android and iOS platforms, for communication purposes; being a member of some associations, all of which were founded and operated within the existing laws and regulations; having worked in some private institutions such as schools, dormitories and media organizations close to the Gülen movement.

News stories as well as the victim statements demonstrated that arbitrariness was prevalent during the trials. Not all those who had money or deposited money in Bank Asya, but those who were filed as having dissenting views were prosecuted. Not all those who sent their children to the schools close to the Gülen movement but only those who were known to have opposed the government and raised their voices against the embezzlement and authoritarian tendencies of the government were prosecuted. Not all of the employees in the closed companies or institutions, but those who were seen as dissidents were punished. Looking at those who were sentenced, different heavy penal courts in different parts of the country gave inconsistent decisions by relying on the same criteria. While some Bank Asya depositors, who were labeled as dissidents, were punished with "aiding a terrorist organization", senior managers at that bank was made the Chairman of the Capital Markets Board and the general manager of human resources at the Central Bank. While many teachers and academics working in private schools and universities were sentenced to prison for membership of a terrorist organization, some continued to work in public or private institutions of their choice. While some people may be fired from their jobs under the pretext of a security investigation just because their father, mother or siblings were expelled with statutory decrees, or they are not employed at all, others have retained their jobs or even got promoted. Even those who were bedridden in the hospital or on vacation on July 15, 2016, or even those who previously died or martyred were included in the putschist/terrorist lists.

46 *Presumption of guilt*

In judicial or administrative proceedings, courts adopted the presumption of guilt instead of presumption of innocence and based their decisions on the rule that the accused are terrorists until they prove their innocence instead of the principle that courts must take the side of an accused party when there are doubts about the charges.

Although it is stated in the 4th paragraph of Article 38 of the Constitution, "Until the guilt is proven…" and the Article 6/2 of the ECHR entrenched that "Everyone charged with a criminal offense shall be presumed innocent until proven guilty according to law," these universal principles were ignored and the state, which was accusing part, benefited from the suspicion. The defendants tried in heavy penal courts were considered criminals/terrorists until they proved their innocence. Those who could not prove their innocence in a way that would convince the adjudicating judge were considered guilty and sentenced to the heaviest punishments, with trivial excuses that had no place in the law.

47 *Violation of rights to defense or to access defense*

The right to defense or access to the defense has been violated by preventing meetings with lawyers through bans, restrictions, threats, harassment or arrests. The Article 6-d of the Decree Law No 667, for instance, stated that attorney/client interviews could be held under the surveillance of the guards and while being recorded with cameras. Victims who objected to this practice were subjected to ill-treatment after their lawyers left.

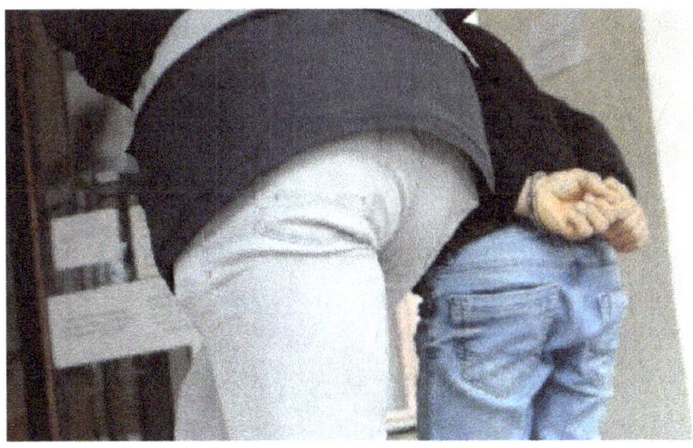

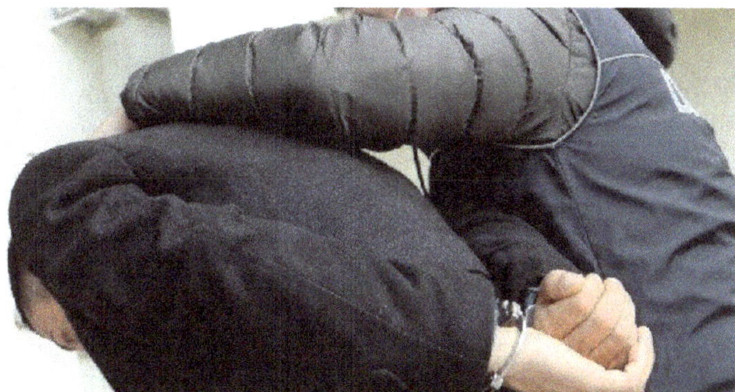

inceleme bölümünde yer alan bilgi, belge, olgu ve tespitler dikkate alındığında;

Her ne kadar başvurucu hakkında Mersin Cumhuriyet Başsavcılığı tarafından kovuşturmaya yer olmadığına karar verilmiş ise de; başvurucunun örgütle irtibatı ve iltisakı bulunduğu yönündeki kurum görüşü başvurucunun FETÖ/PDY örgütüyle irtibatını ortaya koymaktadır

 ## Arbitrary restriction of freedom

The freedoms of the KHK victims were arbitrarily and systematically restricted. For instance, the Law on Criminal Procedures (CMK) affirms the universal principle that arrests should be made in exceptional cases. However, in the trials of the KHK victims and the persons accused of belonging to the Hizmet movement, arrest decisions were frequently made. After the trials, some defendants were convicted. However, while the executions were being carried out, the judicial steps and especially the Supreme Court process were arbitrarily long. In the meantime, the execution periods of many prisoners were already long overdue and many prisoners were unlawfully kept in prisons, stripped of their freedoms on the grounds that the Supreme Court process was still ongoing.

 ## Unsubstantiated allegations

The existence of suspicion of crime was accepted as sufficient evidence of the guilt of the defendants who are tried as part of the persecution under the OHAL/KHK regime. Judicial or administrative courts didn't ask for concrete evidence to base their decisions on in many hearings.

During trials against dissidents and the members of the Gülen movement, the understanding that "it is not imperative to provide undeniable evidence for crimes against the state and in such circumstances, the accuser will benefit from doubt," was adopted. In the presence of even the slightest doubt about the person's affiliation with the Hizmet movement, the rule that a person should not be employed in the public sector was instituted as a state policy. Also measures were taken to prevent them from finding a job in the private sector. This policy started with the Decree Law No. 667 dated 22/7/2016 and has been implemented by all judicial and administrative institutions, including the Constitutional Court, which is the last authority in terms of domestic remedies.

50 *Restriction of complaints and defense rights*

The ways of defending and seeking rights have been blocked for the KHK victims. For instance, the state institutions issued orders to administrations and prosecutors' offices not to take positive action against any application by persons who have been included in any KHK. It has been observed that not a single piece of evidence, information and document has been included in the indictments in favor of the KHK victims during the trials. During these unlawful proceedings of the judiciary and the courts, the rights of the victims have always been accepted absolutely non-existent, the rights of defense have been usurped in an organized manner, and the victims were left confined in a maze with no way out.

51 *Retrospective laws*

The principle of legality that assures that no defendant may be punished arbitrarily or retroactively by the state have been deliberately ignored. People were sentenced to penalties starting from 6 years and 3 months for acts that were not defined as crimes in the law by the time they were performed. Hundreds of thousands of people have been prosecuted for legal rights and activities such as working in a private teaching institution, depositing money in a bank, sending their child to a school approved by the Ministry of National Education, volunteering for an association approved by the governor's office, and organizing a charity sale, all of which were totally legal by the time when the accused did them. Worse, for these normal acts, people were charged with terrorism.

52 *Ignoring the principle of individual criminal responsibility*

Instead of the principle of individual criminal responsibility, the archaic interpretation of "the whole group is responsible for the crime of the individual" has been adopted, and in this direction, allegations and punishments have been issued in a way that extends to the family members and social circles of the persecuted. In one instance, for example, the father of a dismissed person was expelled from where he has been working for years. In another example, the passport of a person was revoked on the grounds that his wife was dismissed from her job by one of the KHKs.

53 *Specially authorized courts*

The right to fair trial was obstructed with 'specially appointed judges - specially designated special authorized courts' that replaced the 'natural judge - natural court'. Specially authorized heavy penal courts were set as per the decisions of the HSK, not by law. Criminal judgeships are judgeships, not courts, and do not fall under the principle of natural judgment.

54 *Sentencing beforehand and looking for evidence later*

Courts ruled punishments for KHK victims and dissidents arbitrarily on the basis of a practice that can be summarized as "punish first, then investigate the situation and look for evidence that may be used as an excuse for punishment'. Indictments were prepared against the defendants 1,5 and 2 years after they were arrested. Tens of thousands of people were only able to learn about the accusations against them after 2 years in prison, and long detention turned into a punishment. Those who were found not guilty after spending up to 3 years in detention were acquitted and released without compensation.

55 Holding family members hostage

When a person victimized by a KHK could not be reached when they were wanted as part of investigations, another family member was taken into custody instead of them. This was confessed directly to the relatives who were taken into custody as hostages. Threats like "If your spouse/child does not surrender, you will remain in detention. Tell him to surrender and so that we will let you go" were made to their faces.

56 Deadlock between the commission and the project courts

A vicious cycle of unlawfulness and arbitrariness was in effect in order to block the path of solution for the KHK victims. Tens of thousands of victims had to wait 3-4 years for the 'accept/reject' decisions of the State of Emergency Commission in order to file a lawsuit at the administrative courts to be able to return to work. Under the control of the government, the commission was rejecting around 95 percent of the applications. The only path of appeal for the victims was to apply to one of the 6 specially designed judgeships in Ankara, which were also under the government's influence and was notoriously used to suppress the opposition as per the orders of the government, particularly of Erdoğan. The suspects had no right to use the ordinary method of applying for appeal to the administrative court closest to their residence. One of the most striking examples of the lawlessness cycle is that of the military school students, who were sentenced to life imprisonment. Although their rights were usurped by the KHK, they could not apply to the OHAL Commission, which is the starting level of domestic remedies, and they could not seek their rights.

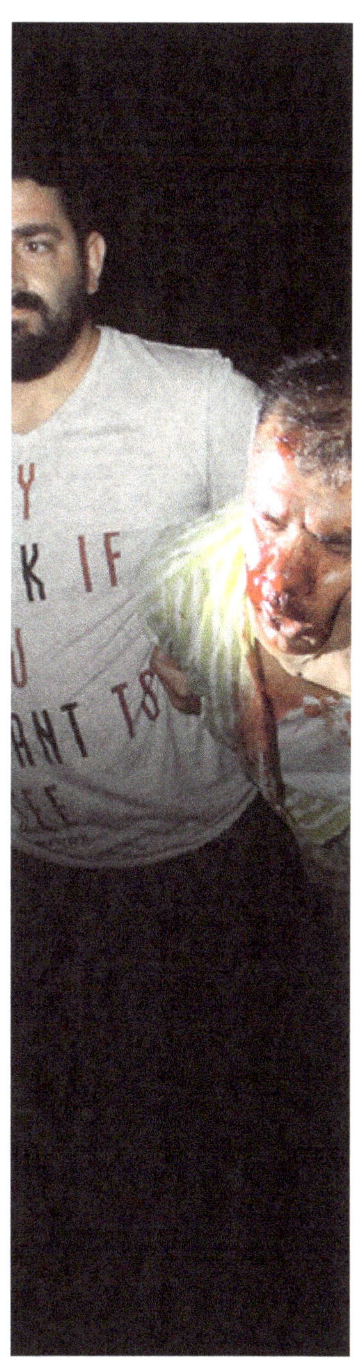

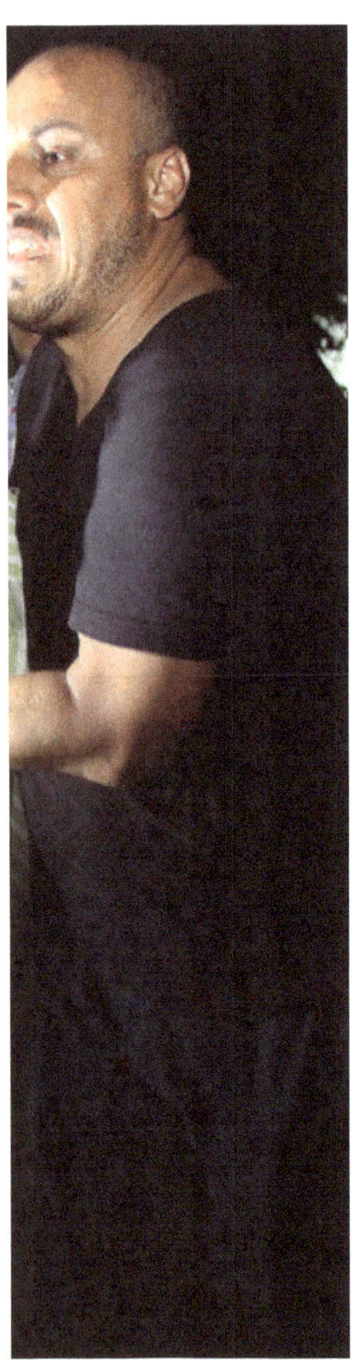

57 *Ill-treatment in detention and under arrest*

KHK victims have been subjected to unlawful detentions and arrests, as well as systematic ill-treatment. Hundreds of suspects were kept in bad conditions in sports halls, as there was no place in police stations and security buildings big enough to house mass arrests of this size. Deliberate and systematic restrictions were put in action in prisons in areas like education, health, sports, communication, life rights as well as a big variety of social activities, which were already naturally limited. Through discriminatory practices and threats, they were forced to confess, to slander people they did not know, to admit events or acts they did not witness, or to make false statements.

58 *Discrimination in penalty relief and forcing to give up legal rights*

Political prisoners faced arbitrary obstacles in enjoying certain legal rights, such as reductions in their execution times. For example, those detained for criminal offenses such as murder, theft and violence against women serve half of their sentences in prison, while those detained for political reasons must spend at least three quarters of their sentence in prison. There is also deliberate long-term detention and coercion to renounce legal rights.

59 Political pressure on judicial and administrative institutions

There was pressure on judicial and administrative institutions to always take their decisions against the KHK victims. Some judges have even reportedly said "I am arresting innocent people. If I do not arrest them, I will end up in prison. I cannot sleep out of guilt." For instance, Fatih Mehmet Aksoy, President of the Kırşehir Heavy Penal Court, was dismissed by the HSK while the trial about a group of police officers was still going on, because he did not give the decision requested from him at the trial despite the prosecutor's threat that he will be arrested over charges of using the ByLock app. In many other cases, Erdoğan's lawyers participated in the trials of KHK victims and exerted pressure on judges and prosecutors.

60 Failure to comply with judicial decisions in favor of the victim

A decision by the European Court of Human Rights in favor of politicians, writers and rights defenders, demanding their release due to unjust detention was ignored. Similarly, the decisions of acquittal or non-prosecution given by the high courts were ignored by the lower courts.

61 Alienating victims in prison

After being convicted without a fair trial and thrown into prisons, the KHK victims and, in broader terms, the members of the Gülen movement faced marginalization in prisons. They were tagged as FETÖ members and were subjected to othering. In the closed visit table prepared by the prison execution boards and announced on the website, there is a tag "TF ÜST (FETÖ)" in bold next to the names of some wards.

The Right to Property

- ▷ **Extortion of property rights**
- ▷ **Extortion of financial rights**
- ▷ **Extortion of pension rights**
- ▷ **Extortion of individual savings**
- ▷ **Extortion of the right of inheritance**
- ▷ **Prohibition of sale of personal property**
- ▷ **The usurpation of the rights on real estate**
- ▷ **The usurpation of the rights on the movables**
- ▷ **Blocking of bank accounts**

62 *Extortion of property rights*

The victims' property rights were confiscated and they were asked to pay rent to be able to stay in their own property. The receivables of the KHK victims or members of the Hizmet movement have not been paid. Even some people got encouraged by this attitude of the state and looted the property of the KHK victims similar to the state's plunder while some refused to pay their debts to these people. As an example to this violation, all the assets of Akın İpek and his family, as well as the universities, schools and dormitories they built for charity, were confiscated. Melek İpek, Akın İpek's mother, was demanded to pay rent to be able to continue staying in her own house.

63 *Extortion of financial rights*

The financial rights of the KHK victims earned retroactively due to their profession such as remuneration, accrued additional course fees, etc. have been usurped. Some of them were even asked to pay their salaries retrospectively.

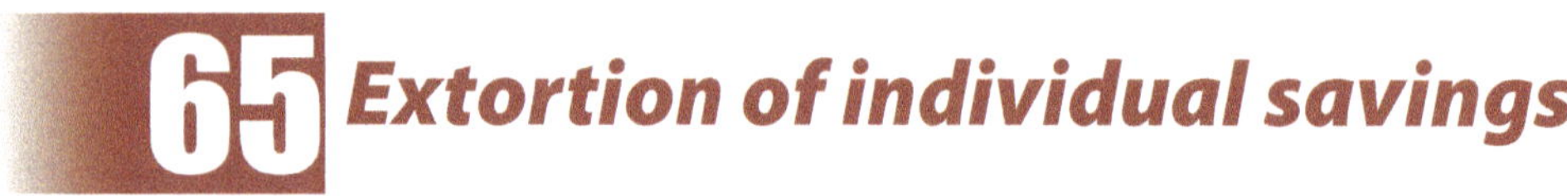

64 Extortion of pension rights

People who were legally entitled with pensions, including disability pensions, were arbitrarily prevented from retiring. Thus, their right to receive pension premiums has been extorted. The Article 50 of the Law No. 7194, published in the Official Gazette on 7 December 2019, the arbitrary practices against the SGK employees were taken under legal protection, allowing this tool of economic genocide to become systematic.

65 Extortion of individual savings

Some victims' savings in private funds were blocked, dispossessing them of their contingency livelihoods after losing their income sources.

66 Extortion of the right of inheritance

The property of the KHK victims was confiscated by preventing them from benefiting from their families' inheritance. The entries of the victims were encoded in the land registry cadastral records with the code of "risky person" and the right to inherit in the future was usurped.

67 Prohibition of sale of personal property

A significant number of KHK victims were prevented from selling their properties like house, land, etc. as a result of the 'risky person' code the state put in their registration records in the database of the General Directorate of Land Registry/Cadastre.

68 *The usurpation of the rights on real estate*

The right of use of the KHK victims on their real estate has been usurped. For example, an 87-year-old woman, Sıttıka Atay, donated her house to a foundation that was closed by statutory decree, to be transferred after her death. However, the public institution that took over this foundation with this decree, filed a lawsuit and took the ownership of the old woman's house before she died. Although it was written in the title deed that 'the right of usufruct belongs to Sıttıka Atay', they seized the house where Atay had lived for 65 years, while she was still alive, as if she had no right to dispose of her property, and made her an 'occupant' in her own property.

69 *The usurpation of the rights on the movables*

Profiled in the databases of almost all of the state institutions and electronic government services as objectionable or risky persons, KHK victims were rendered unable to sell their securities holdings due to the obstacles placed in their way.

70 *Blocking of bank accounts*

BDDK and criminal courts of peace blocked the bank accounts of many dissidents, restricting their access to their savings. They were prevented from using their savings when they needed it most after losing their jobs as if they were condemned to hunger and despair with their families.

The rights of citizenship, participation and benefitting from public services

▷ Denial of the right to vote and be elected
▷ Assault on civil servants' administrative rights and assets
▷ Deprivation from citizenship rights at embassies
▷ Prohibition of using social facilities
▷ Prohibition from using funeral services
▷ Prevention from participation in civil society
▷ Prevention from entering school buildings
▷ Preventing them from taking their personal belongings from their workplaces
▷ Prevention from renting a car
▷ Preventing blood donation
▷ Obstruction of maternity benefits
▷ Obstruction of maternity entitlement allowance
▷ Blocking the right to Short-Time Working Allowance
▷ Exception from the ban on dismissal
▷ Banned from epidemic aid
▷ Exclusion from the protection of the dismissal ban brought during the pandemic process
▷ Deprivation of support provided to tradesmen and craftsmen during the pandemic process
▷ The usurpation of citizenship rights obtained through marriage bond
▷ Prevention of benefiting from Health Insurance services
▷ Prevention of receiving disability pension
▷ Prevention of pensions for care
▷ Prevention of natural disaster relief
▷ Prevention of the companion's pension
▷ Denial of social and economic support rights

71 Denial of the right to vote and be elected

Some politicians came up with an offer to prohibit certain opposition groups and the people known to have links with the Gülen movement from voting, attempting to deprive a significant part of the people of the right to elect and be elected, one of the most integral citizenship rights. On the other hand, the candidates who won the municipal elections, especially in the regions where Kurdish voters are concentrated, were not given their mandates or were dismissed due to lawsuits brought against them after taking office, and officers loyal to Erdoğan were appointed as trustees to replace these mayors. Likewise, although they were elected, some of the municipal committees or headmen were not given their mandates.

72 Denial of the right to vote and be elected

KHK victims have been ignored in the institutions they work for. Contrary to even the current decree laws, their superiors in public institutions arbitrarily implemented procedures such as suspension and dismissal as 'administrative decisions' against the KHK victims, who were reinstituted to their positions later.

73 Deprivation from citizenship rights at embassies

Embassies and consulates did not prepare or approve the documents the dissidents abroad demanded for their judicial and administrative proceedings in Turkey. When victims who cannot receive notary services from embassies or consulates use the internationally valid 'Apostille' mechanism, their transactions were deemed invalid. In a similar fashion, Turkish embassies and consulates also refused to provide the necessary documents when dissidents living abroad applied for family reunification visas.

74 *Prohibition of using social facilities*

The burial of some deceased KHK victims in the cemeteries was not allowed. In addition to not performing religious/humane duties such as gasil [washing and cleaning the corpse], shrouding in white cloth and burying with prayers, the victims were even prevented from being provided with a transport vehicle when they died.

Gökhan Açıkkollu, who died as a result of torture in detention, was intended to be buried in a land designated and called as "the traitors cemetery". As a result of his family's struggle, Açıkkollu's dead body was taken to his wife's town, however, the officially appointed imam of the mosque there did not want to lead the funeral prayer of the deceased and the family had to carry out the burial procession by themselves. The investigation against Açıkkollu cleared him after his death and the state ordered his reinstatement to his teaching role 1.5 years after his murder. The officers who killed him by torture were not punished.

75 *Prohibition from using funeral services*

During their travels across the country, KHK victims wanted to stay in social facilities like public guest houses which are much less expensive, safer and cleaner compared to many alternative accommodation places. However, they were not allowed to stay in these guest houses, and they were even chased away by facility administrations, who said "no terrorist is allowed here."

76 Prevention from participation in civil society

The social existence and status of the victims were almost annihilated by preventing them from participating in associations and foundations as members. The KHK victims were even prevented from being members of school-parent unions or the neighborhood mosque associations.

77 Prevention from entering school buildings

Academics and teachers who were expelled by KHKs were forbidden from entering the school buildings and their right to education was taken from them.

78 Preventing them from taking their personal belongings from their workplaces

Expelled teachers could not even take their personal belongings from their lockers because they were forbidden to enter the school buildings where they used to work.

 79 Prevention from renting a car

There have been instances where they were not even allowed to rent a car despite paying their fees.

 80 Preventing blood donation

The Red Crescent rejected the applications of some of the KHK victims who wanted to donate blood.

 81 Obstruction of maternity benefits

Some KHK victims were not allowed to enjoy maternity benefits, one of the basic civil rights recognized by citizenship.

82 *Obstruction of maternity entitlement allowance*

The 'maternity entitlement allowance', which is paid after giving birth to every Turkish citizen woman who meets the conditions, was not delivered to KHK victims.

83 *Blocking the right to Short-Time Working Allowance*

The government has extended short-time working allowance for employers as they had to stop operation at their workplaces or whose work was interrupted for a short time due to the Coronavirus epidemic. However, some employers who hired KHK victims were not allowed to benefit from this allowance.

84 *Denial of epidemic aid*

Those who were expelled by KHKs applied to the ministry to benefit from the aid of TL 1,000 per person, which will be given within the scope of the COVID 19 epidemic measures. Their application was turned down on the grounds that any person who was directly affected by KHKs cannot get benefits from the social state.

85 Exclusion from the protection of the dismissal ban brought during the pandemic process

Employers exploited the difficulty of KHK victims of finding a job elsewhere, making them work without compulsory insurance records. The state has implemented a number of measures to ameliorate the negative effects of the pandemic conditions on the business world and the labor market. These measures included a ban on layoffs during the pandemic. Some companies, whose business slowed down or stopped during the pandemic period, dismissed the KHK victims that they employed unregistered.

86 Deprivation of support provided to tradesmen and craftsmen during the pandemic process

Persons who were able to open a business after being dismissed from public service with the Decree Laws who wanted to benefit from the direct income or grant support given to the tradesmen due to the COVID 19 epidemic applied to the Ministry of Family and Social Services. The ministry rejected the support applications on the pretext that the applicants were expelled by decree.

87 The usurpation of citizenship rights obtained through marriage bond

The Ministry of Interior rejected the citizenship application of a spouse with KHK, on the grounds that "the necessity of examining the application conditions stipulated in the legislation not only for the applicant, but also in a way that covers both spouses is a result of the sovereignty of the state in citizenship. " This refusal decision was upheld by the administrative court.

88 Prevention of benefiting from Health Insurance services

Those who were expelled from the public sector and exposed to the genocide practice lost their right to benefit from general health insurance (GSS) services. Therefore, they were prevented from receiving health services. The families of the victims were exposed to risks such as death, permanent health damage and they were prevented from living a healthy life.

89 *Prevention of receiving disability pension*

The disability pension, which was paid to every disabled citizen of the Republic of Turkey who met the conditions, was not given to the victims of the Decree Law, and thus their basic rights were usurped.

90 *Prevention of pensions for care*

The care pension, which was paid to every citizen of the Republic of Turkey who met the conditions, was not given to the KHK victims and thus their basic rights were usurped.

91 *Prevention of natural disaster relief*

Natural disaster relief, which was paid to every citizen of the Republic of Turkey who met the conditions, was not given to the KHK victims and their basic rights were usurped.

92 *Prevention of the companion's pension*

The companion allowance, which is paid to the people who took care of the patient who is treated at a hospital, was not given to the KHK victims. Thus, another of their rights was usurped or blocked.

93 *Denial of social and economic support rights*

Social and economic support provided to every citizen of the Republic of Turkey who met the conditions was not given to families of the KHK victims. The state's excluding the KHK victims and dissidents, which it had condemned to starvation by closing all their livelihoods, from social assistance was one of the severe social genocide practices.

Right to Form a Family, Residence and Private Life

▷ **Preventing establishing a family**
▷ **Forcing to divorce**
▷ **Forcing children to reject their parents**
▷ **Forcing parents to reject their children**
▷ **Separation of children from their families**
▷ **Separation of adoptees from their families**
▷ **Breaking up families by destroying their social bonds**
▷ **Breaking up families by usurping their right to education**
▷ **The destruction of the structural functionality of families**
▷ **Forced evacuation and immigration**
▷ **Forcing tenants to evict**
▷ **Refusal of house rental requests**

94 *Preventing establishing a family*

Due to social, economic and psychological pressures, many young people who were preparing for marriage could not get married. Marriages did not take place due to the obstacles of families, relatives or society, and sometimes because official institutions did not provide the necessary documents for marriage.

95 *Forcing to divorce*

The victims had to separate from their spouses due to the pressures they faced from their families and relatives. Even in the courts, the judges themselves encouraged the spouses of those who were prosecuted for being a member of the Hizmet movement, to divorce. According to the data provided by the Turkish Statistics Institution (TurkStat) for 2019, divorce rates among victim families were found to be 17-20 times higher than the Turkey average. When the families that are not legally divorced but living separately are included, it is seen that this rate corresponds to 60 times the average of Turkey.

96 Forcing children to reject their parents

The unity of the families of the KHK victims was damaged by forcing the children of the KHK victims to reject their parents. For example, Hümeyra Nur Tekalan Toman, daughter of the former rector of Fatih University, Şerif Ali Tekalan, said, "he is only my biological father."

97 Forcing parents to reject their children

Some parents disowned their children who were targeted by the political power. For example, Mehmet Uğur Erdil applied to the Mersin Family Court to disown his two sons, who were dismissed from their duties and forced to retire as part of the investigations into the Gülen movement. The court rejected the application, arguing that there was no serious crime. The father said, "even though the court did not accept my application, I disowned them both because they were parallelists [a term Erdoğan was using to denote the members of the Gülen movement in the public sector]."

98 *Separation of children from their families*

The children of the KHK victim parents, who were detained or arrested, were given to other persons or to the Child Protection Agency by order of the prosecutor's office.

99 *Separation of adoptees from their families*

Fatma Betül Kaya, the former Minister of Family and Social Policies, ordered on August 23 that the adopted children be taken back from families known to have affiliations with the Gülen movement within the framework of the government instructions to take every precaution in the efforts to exterminate the movement. Thus, children who struggled with the trauma of losing their birth parents were victimized for the second time by a similar trauma of bereavement. Parents were also devastated. According to the laws, the foster family status is canceled if it is determined that the child is neglected and abused, exposed to ill-treatment, the behavior of the family contrary to the social values is observed, the physical and mental health of the family is documented, or it is determined that the family is not in effective communication with the institution.

100 Breaking up families by destroying their social bonds

There were attempts to harass and break up families by severing their social ties. The parents were declared undesirable by the other parents because they were expelled by KHKs. They were prevented from attending parent meetings where they could talk about their children's issues.

101 Breaking up families by usurping their right to education

Children whose parents have been dismissed by the decree laws were prevented from settling in the private schools or universities they had won. They were also prevented from receiving the degrees they had earned. After their or their children's education rights were usurped, in some families, individuals blamed each other, which led to the disintegration of family unity.

102 The destruction of the structural functionality of families

Detention, which is normally used exceptionally, is applied to both parents at the same time, without considering the children, even if there is even a slight suspicion of affiliation with the Hizmet movement. In some cases, some members of the families were arbitrarily given punishments such as travel restrictions and house arrest. Sometimes, when the person wanted for detention could not be found, other members of the family were taken into custody as hostages. All these practices have seriously damaged the unity, harmony and functionality of many families.

103 Forced evacuation and immigration

The KHK victims were forced to leave their lodgings allocated to them by the institution they work for on short notice. For example, judges and prosecutors, who were dismissed from their profession without even getting their defense, were asked to evacuate their lodgings within 15 days.

104 Forcing tenants to evict

Tenants of the victims, who have rental income from their houses and workplaces, were forced to move to other places by threats or pressures such as 'you cannot stay in that terrorist's house/workplace and make him money'.

105 Refusal of house rental requests

The KHK victims, who were expelled from their places of residence, were forced to hide their identities when they moved to another place. Otherwise, their applications for rental houses were rejected.

The Right to Education and Self-Development

- ▷ Obstruction of university education
- ▷ Prohibition of special talents from special education
- ▷ Cutting off educational scholarships
- ▷ Cutting off of private school scholarships
- ▷ Preventing applications for education scholarships
- ▷ Preventing participation in state-sponsored projects
- ▷ Denial of the right to be an athlete

106 Obstruction of university education

KHK Victims and even sometimes their relatives were not admitted to undergraduate, graduate and doctorate programs they won or deserved.

107 Prohibition of special talents from special education

The right of the gifted children of the KHK victims to receive education after successfully passing the exams for determining the talents in and their selection has been canceled on the grounds that they are relatives of the KHK victims.

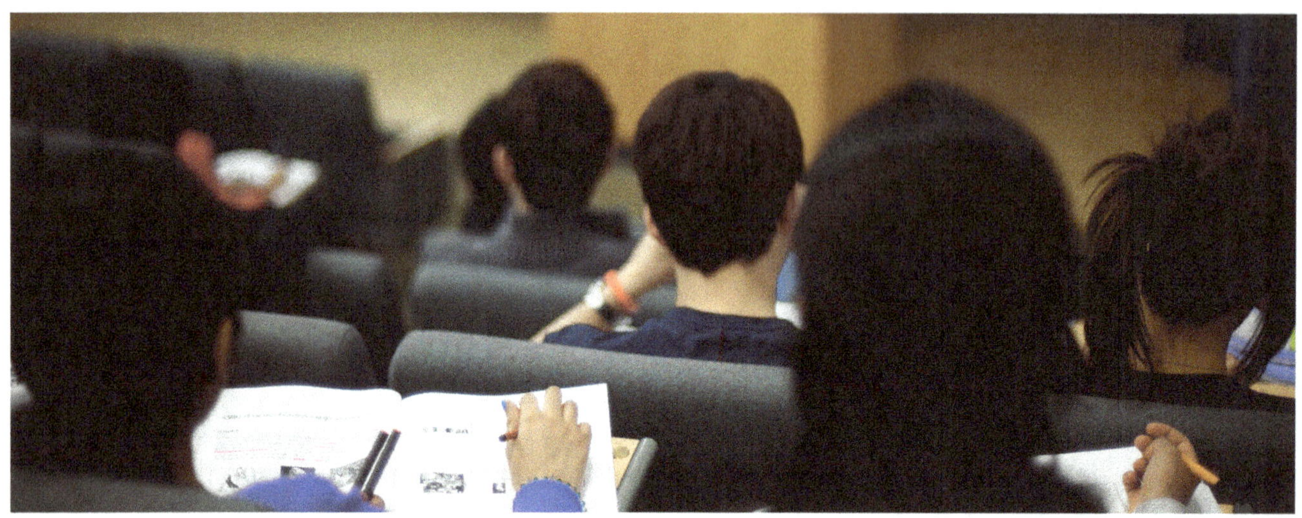

108 Cutting off educational scholarships

Ongoing education scholarships of students at home and abroad have been ceased. In some cases, these students were even asked to pay back the money they had received until then, with interest accrued. For example, on March 24, 2020, the education loans of 2 university students were cut by the General Directorate of Credits and Dormitories under the Ministry of Youth and Sports, as per a directive of the Ankara Police Department, and would be taken back with legal interest. Similar practices have been experienced in other provinces, in many institutions such as the Ministry of National Education and the Scientific and Technological Research Council of Turkey (TÜBİTAK).

109 Cutting off of private school scholarships

The student scholarship rights of the children of KHK victims and their families who study with scholarships in private schools or who are entitled to enroll in private schools with scholarships due to their high success in the placement exams have been arbitrarily denied or usurped. These usurpations of rights were made through the lists of the Ministry of National Education Information Systems (MEBBİS) or e-Government, which were prepared in an unknown manner and kept from the public.

110 Preventing applications for education scholarships

The children of the KHK victims were barred from the education and training support scholarships provided by the state institutions. When students apply for dormitories or scholarships, they are asked to give 'a commitment that no terrorism investigation or expulsion has been made against any of their relatives'. Thus, their application was blocked. When the applicants applied by hiding their contact with any relative that was expelled by the KHKs, their scholarships were not awarded again on the grounds that they made false statements.

111 Preventing participation in state-sponsored projects

Academicians and students, whose names were in a KHK, were prevented from participating in all state-sponsored scientific projects in any capacity be it as students, interns or researchers.

112 Denial of the right to be an athlete

Children of KHK victims have been removed from or not included in sports teams/clubs of which they are members.

The Right to Health, Social Security and Solidarity

- ▷ Being deprived of social security services
- ▷ Preventing solidarity and helping each other
- ▷ Establishing a confrontational culture based on suspicion, denunciation, harassment and lynching
- ▷ Prohibition of benefiting from social and religious solidarity
- ▷ Criminalization of moral support
- ▷ Prevention of social relations
- ▷ Arresting those helping to find a job

 113 *Being deprived of social security services*

Health insurance rights and material and moral guarantees of the KHK victims and their relatives have been arbitrarily usurped with the codes 36 or 38, which denoted that the person in question was expelled by a KHK, in the records of the Social Security Institution. Thus, they were prevented from benefiting from the services that the social state promised to provide to its citizens, causing many people to die or commit suicide due to neglect, malnutrition and stress.

114 *Preventing solidarity and helping each other*

All social assistance activities, including aid and support provided to the victims by their family members and relatives, were blocked. Aids made by social solidarity associations or individuals were prevented. Any financial or moral assistance to the KHK victims or to families whose livelihoods have been closed because they are members of the Hizmet movement has been considered as 'support to terrorism'. Those who were found to be helping in this way were arrested and imprisoned.

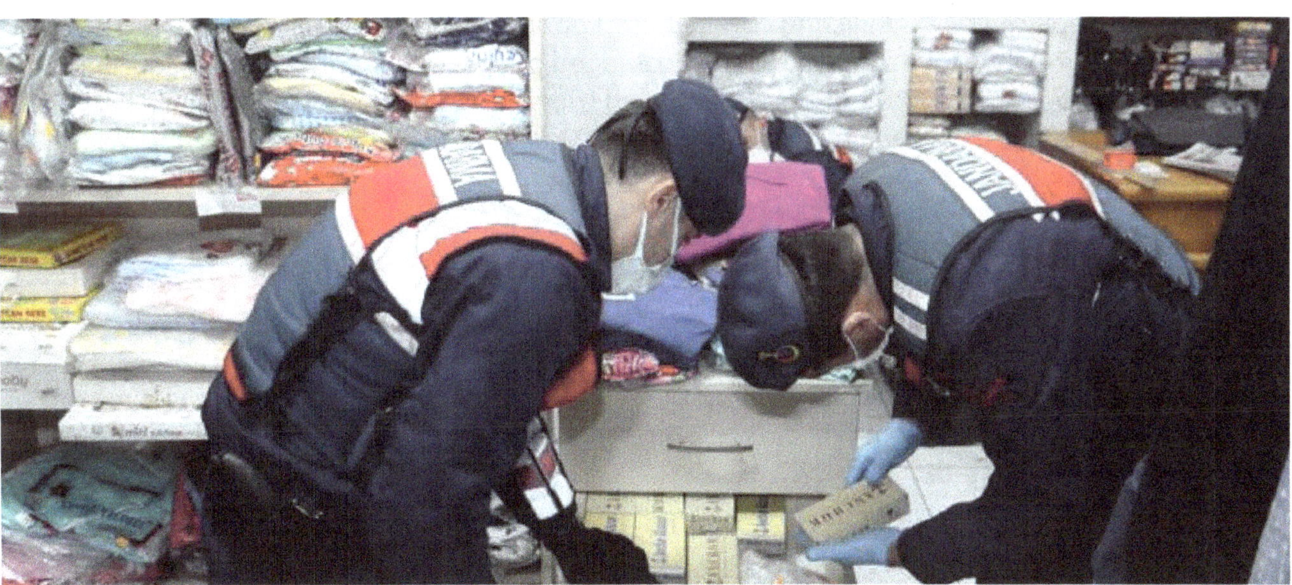

FETÖ/PDY Silahlı Terör Örgütünün başarısız darbe girişiminden sonra il
yeniden yapılanması sürecinde Mağdur Aile Yapılanması kapsamında faaliyet g
değerlendirilen ________________, FETÖ/PDY kapsamında hakkında adli işlem kaydı
kişilerle irtibatını kesmediği, onlara dualar ederek örgüt üyelerine manevi olarak
destek olmaya çalışıp örgüt üyelerinin morallerini en üst seviyede tutmaya çalış
davranışından ________________'ın örgüt üyesi olduğu ve örgüte olan inancının halen deva
değerlendirilmiştir.

TAPE-5

115 Establishing a confrontational culture based on suspicion, denunciation, harassment and lynching

Among the people, the traditional culture of solidarity, neighborliness and benevolence was
destroyed and replaced by a conflicting culture based on suspicion, denunciation, harassment
and lynching. Through the media, politicians encouraged people to denounce their neighbors,
friends and relatives. The spirit of unity, solidarity and trust among the people has been deliberately
destroyed, and people have been polarized.

116 Prohibition of benefiting from social and religious solidarity

Religious aids like fitra and zakat alms were prevented from being given to the KHK victims or
those who were labeled as members of the Hizmet movement. Those who tried to extend such
aids covertly were arrested.

Criminalization of moral support

Even the meeting of the KHK victims with each other and their moral support to each other caused investigations against them. For example, a few KHK victims, who met and had a picnic after being released from prison in Kayseri, were detained by the police. Similarly, the picnic held by university students, whose parents were KHK victims, in İstanbul for the purpose of meeting and solidarity has been the subject of investigation.

In another example, the Chief Public Prosecutor's Office in Ordu province accused a man of praying and providing moral support to the members of the Gülen movement. Arguing that praying for them shows that that person is also a member of the movement and that his belief in the organization still continues, the prosecution opened an investigation against the person.

Prevention of social relations

Human relations such as neighborhood, friendship and solidarity were tried to be prevented and destroyed. For example, an indictment prepared by the Ordu Chief Public Prosecutor's Office accepted a person's routine actions such as visiting a sick person or taking a bicycle tire for repair as evidence that the unity among the members of the Gülen movement continues and that they are trying to support each other materially and morally. The office started an investigation for membership in a terrorist organization about that person.

Arresting those helping to find a job

Persons or institutions that helped the KHK victims to find a job were accused of supporting terrorism. Friends and relatives who found jobs for the victims for the sake of solidarity were detained and arrested.

Right to Work and Doing Business

- ▷ Extensive purges in the public sector and barring from public service
- ▷ Extensive purges in the private sector and obstacles in working life
- ▷ Denial of the right to work
- ▷ Prohibition of working in new or different jobs
- ▷ Prohibition of internship
- ▷ Blocking access to economic activity documents
- ▷ Prevention of opening a business, obtaining a license
- ▷ Blocking opening a bank account
- ▷ Blocking bank transfers
- ▷ Rejection of loan requests
- ▷ Refusal of requests to benefit from debt payment facility
- ▷ Cancellation of credit cards
- ▷ Extortion of receivables
- ▷ Rejection of POS device applications
- ▷ Obstruction of the right to tax deduction
- ▷ Obstruction of insurance service

120 Extensive purges in the public sector and barring from public service

Tens of thousands of people have been arbitrarily terminated from their civil service on the grounds of 'affiliation with a terrorist organization' for their alleged ties with the Gülen movement. This practice was not only limited to the victims who are alleged to have committed the crime of 'being a member of the Gülen movement', but was also extended to those who have kinship relations with the arbitrary discrimination under the excuses such as interview and security investigation. These people were dismissed from their jobs in the public sector or were prevented from being appointed to or working in public institutions.

121 Extensive purges in the private sector and obstacles in working life

The social genocide practices were not limited to the public sector, similar practices were also witnessed in the private sector. Victims and their relatives are also prevented from working in private companies that have business relations with public institutions due to codes 36 and 38, which are logged in the SGK records and indicate that they have been dismissed with the KHKs. For example, the first paragraph of Article 4 of the Law on Private Education Institutions stated that the real person founders of private education institutions, their managers, founder representatives and personnel cannot be a member or may not have any kind of affiliation with terrorist organizations or structures, formations or groups determined by the National Security Council to act against the national security of the state.

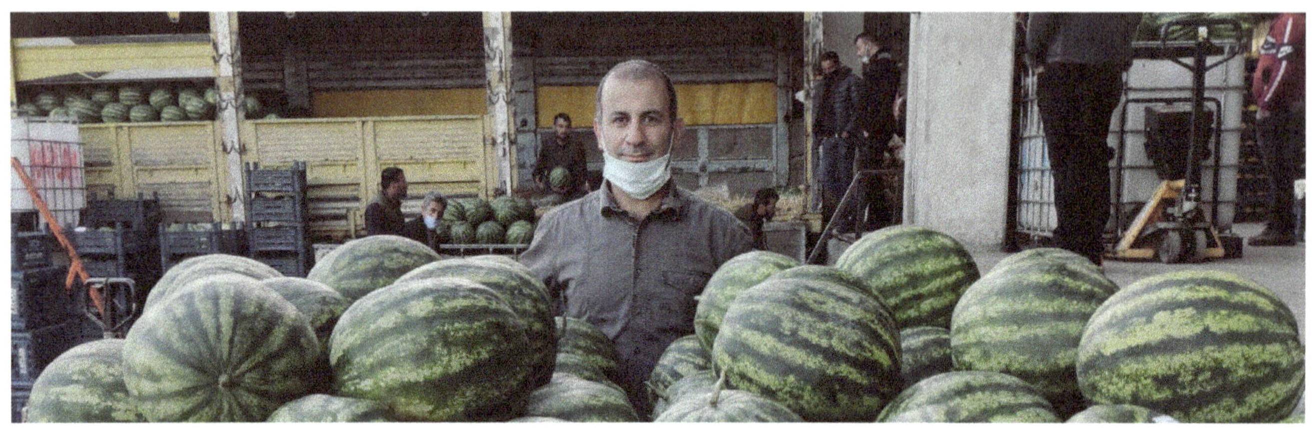

122 — Prohibition of promotion of relatives and descendants of the KHK victims working in the public sector

In addition to the mobbing and harassment practices applied to the relatives of the KHK victims working in the public sector, their promotions were arbitrarily prevented.

123 — Denial of the right to work

With the additional measures included in the decree laws, the rights of the KHK victims to use, renew, extend or obtain new professional licenses have been usurped. In this context, the licenses of teaching, advocacy, private security, piloting, parachuting, seamanship, diving, occupational health and safety, real estate appraisal, Ministry of Finance internal audit, expert witness and sworn translator were revoked. Victims were prevented from practicing their profession, in which they had years of experience, in Turkey or elsewhere in the world, by not being given the license documents and professional certificates they deserved, by not issuing equivalence documents, and by revoking their license or authorization certificates.

124 Prohibition of working in new or different jobs

KHK victims were systematically excluded from new vocational training programs of institutions such as İSMEK, İŞKUR, MEB, Ministry of Health, Ministry of Finance. Thus, it became difficult for them to start a new profession, start a business, and work in a new or different job. It has become very hard for people with code 36 registered in their SGK, İŞKUR and e-government records to enroll in a vocational training course. Those who are already registered were either deregistered or could not get their course completion or professional competency certificates.

125 Prohibition of internship

Internship applications of the KHK victims or their children were rejected.

126 Blocking access to economic activity documents

When the KHK victims wanted to start a commercial enterprise, open a business or get support for their commercial venture, the necessary documents and license applications were arbitrarily rejected. Thus, their commercial enterprise was hindered.

127 Prevention of opening a business, obtaining a license

Those who were able to obtain a business opening license also faced difficulties later. In one example, although the KHK victim's application to open a shop was accepted, it was later blocked. The person who took the permit spent his savings, even loaned money, for the shop he wanted to open, but after making all kinds of expenses, his license was canceled right before the store was about to open. In another example, the same arbitrariness was applied to another KHK victim who wanted to open a health cabin in their hometown.

128 Blocking opening a bank account

Due to the codes numbered 36 and 38 recorded in the e-state and SGK records, the rights of the KHK victims to benefit from banking services were restricted. These persons, who were able to find a job with difficulty during the state of emergency, could not open an account in banks where their salaries would be deposited. Thus, they lost the jobs they had found with difficulty.

129 Blocking bank transfers

KHK mağdurlarına eşleri dahil olmak üzere bazı bankalardan banka havalesi/EFT yaptırılmamıştır. Bu konu ile ilgili yapılan araştırmada bu türden kayıtların genelde BDDK aracılığı ile koydurulduğu anlaşılmaktadır.

130 Rejection of loan requests

Some banks did not allow the KHK victims to use loans.

131 Refusal of requests to benefit from debt payment facility

Some banks have rejected the applications of persons, who had codes with their names in the e-state denoting that they were expelled by KHKs, for payment facilities such as debt restructuring and deferral.

132 Cancellation of credit cards

Some banks canceled the credit cards of the KHK victims.

133 Extortion of receivables

Insurance receivables and commercial receivables of the KHK victims were usurped.

134 Rejection of POS device applications

Banks rejected the POS device requests of those the KHK victims, who wanted to start doing business after they were expelled.

135 Obstruction of the right to tax deduction

Demands for tax reduction by the KHK victims, which is the right of every citizen of the Republic of Turkey, were not accepted.

136 Obstruction of insurance service

The KHK victims could not benefit from the insurance services for which they regularly paid their premiums. Vehicles of the victims were not insured or their right to collect the reparations for the physical damage of the accident was prevented. The insurance cost of the person whose vehicle was damaged in the accident was not paid because a legal action by the KHK was taken against him. About a year after the accident, this insurance company stepped back from the discrimination practice and agreed to pay the damage.

Right to Freedom of Travel

- ▷ **Denial of freedom to travel**
- ▷ **Denial of freedom of movement of descendants**

137 *Denial of freedom to travel*

The freedom of movement of the KHK victims has been taken away. By restricting their freedom to travel abroad, the state prohibited them from working, receiving education, living freely and/or reuniting their families abroad.

138 *Denial of freedom of movement of descendants*

By restricting their freedom to travel abroad, the state prohibited the relatives and descendants of the KHK victims from working, receiving education, living freely and/or reuniting their families abroad.

Women's Rights

▷ **Detention and arrest of pregnant women and women who just gave birth**
▷ **Deaths due to the arrests of pregnant women and women who just gave birth**

139 *Detention and arrest of pregnant women and women who just gave birth*

Pregnant or newly giving birth women who are victims of KHK were arrested for their acts that are not crimes under the law and suffered serious psychological and physical traumas. Dozens of women were taken for interrogation from the delivery room while they were still giving birth. Many of them were sent behind bars with their babies after giving birth, despite the express provision of Article 16/4 of the Law on the Execution of Penalties and Security Measures 5275. The relevant article of the law states: "The execution of the prison sentence against a woman who is pregnant or who gave birth less than six months ago shall be postponed. If the child has died or has been given to someone else, the prison sentence shall begin to be executed two months after the date of birth."

140 *Deaths due to the arrests of pregnant women and women who just gave birth*

Pregnant women, who were arrested despite the clear provision in the law, lost their babies or their own lives in prisons. Some pregnant women have been delayed or prevented from receiving health care even when they are bleeding. These delays and inhibitions have caused the death of the babies in the mother's womb or the death of the mother with her baby.

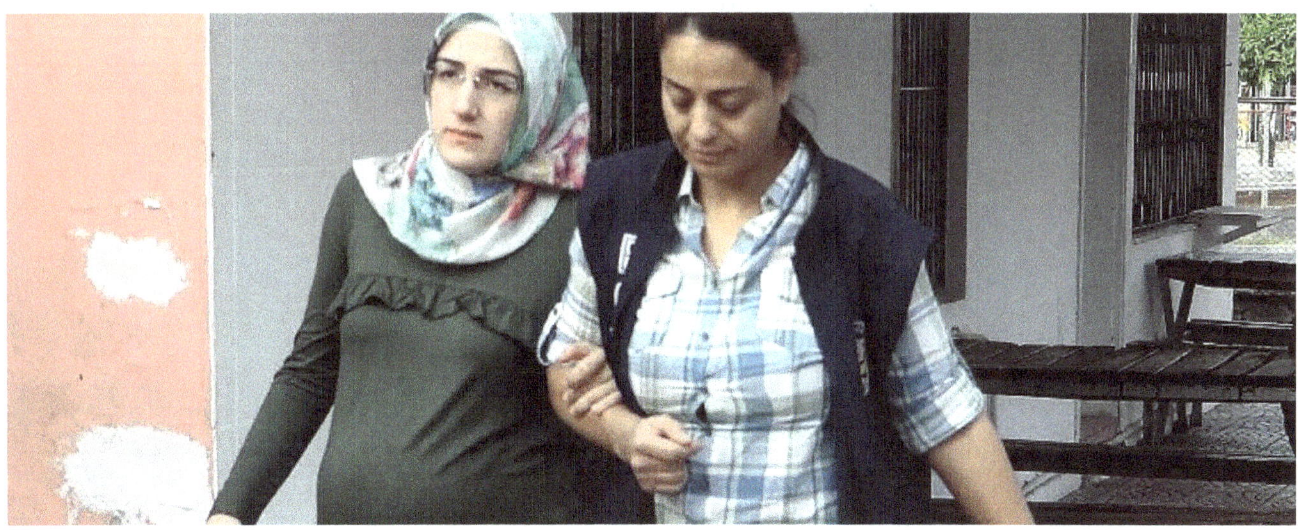

Children's Rights

▷ **Deprivations of infants and young children in prison**
▷ **Imprisonment of children in solitary confinement**
▷ **Deprivation of infants from breast milk**

 141   *Deprivations of infants and young children in prison*

Children who did not have a parent to take care of them due to the detention and arrest of their parents for political reasons were sent to prison with their mothers, and since these children were not given a separate meal and bed, the mothers had to share their own food and a single bed with their child. They were also deprived of very crucial elements for child development, such as playgrounds, toys, communication with peers and nursery.

 142   *Imprisonment of children in solitary confinement*

A KHK victim woman, who asked for the replacement of the formula she ordered for her baby, was accused of disrespectful behavior and was sent to solitary confinement with her baby as punishment.

143   *Deprivation of infants from breast milk*

KHK-victim imprisoned women were separated from their babies, who were still breastfeeding, and had to express their milk in the sink when they could not breastfeed their babies. Some of these women were weaned. In some cases, the baby was brought to prison to suckle his mother twice a day.

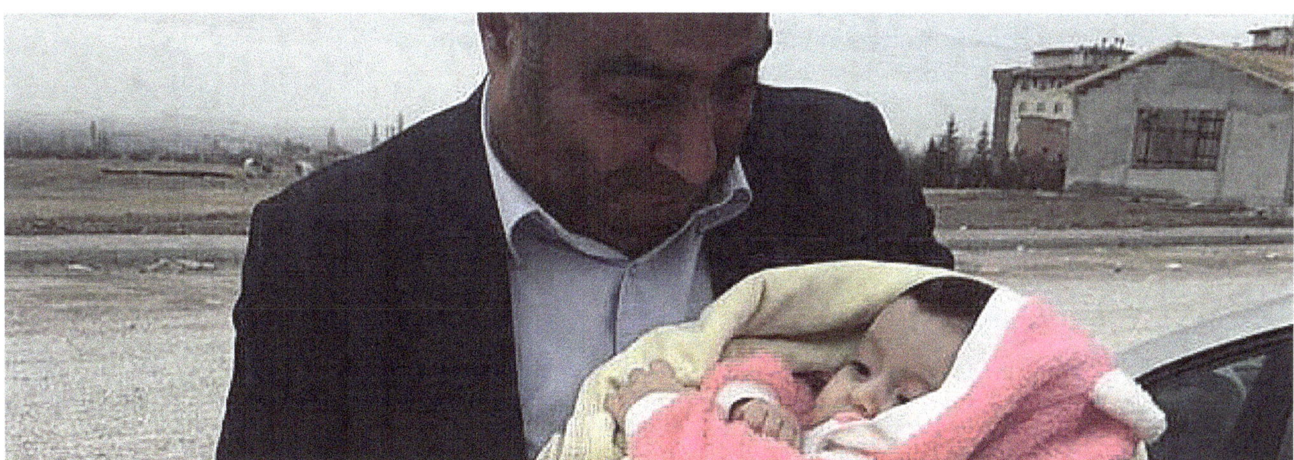

SUPPORT AST

BY MAKING A MONTHLY DONATION OR ONE-TIME DONATION

☑ **CREDIT CARD OR DEBIT**
silencedturkey.org/donatenow

☑ **PAYPAL**
paypal.me/ast111

☑ **ZELLE**
advocatesofsilencedturkey@gmail.com

☑ **PATREON**
patreon.com/advocatesofsilencedturkey

☑ **SEND CHECK**
Please make your checks payable to
"Advocates of Silenced Turkey"
Address: Advocates of Silenced Turkey
P.O. Box 2399 Wayne, NJ 07474-2399

☑ **SUBSCRIBE TO OUR NEWSLETTER**
https://bit.ly/2UEYDwD

☑ help@silencedturkey.org

ADVOCATES OF SILENCED TURKEY

AST is a 501(c)(3) tax exempt, not for profit charitable and educational organization based in New Jersey, USA exclusively for defending human and civil rights.

EIN : 83-1568246

MAILING ADDRESS

Advocates of Silenced Turkey
P.O. Box 2399
Wayne, NJ 07474-2399

CONTACT

help@silencedturkey.org

WEB & SOCIAL MEDIA

www.silencedturkey.org
silencedturkey
facebook.com/silencedturkey
youtube.com/advocatesofsilencedturkey